A Journal of Self-Discovery

THE JOURNEY OF A
WRITTEN LIFE

Kenya Dryden

ISBN (Print): 978-1-09838-304-6
ISBN (eBook): 978-1-09838-305-3

"THE BEST WAY TO MAKE
YOUR DREAMS COME TRUE
IS TO WAKE UP."

Paul Valery

CREATOR'S PLEDGE

I Am a creator.

I Am an expression of the God within me.

I Am divine.

I have a divine right, the power, the ability to create all

things beautiful and to be purposeful.

I Am within what I create outside of myself.

I have dreams that I will make come true.

I Am my journey.

I have the power and strength to travel from experience to experience

by taking action and persevering.

I Am always going to do my best.

I have a role to play in my life.

I Am going to embrace my role.

I deserve the very best in life.

I will always give my best to life.

I Am the action that needs to be taken to create the life that I deserve.

I AM.

LIFE'S NEVER AN EASY JOURNEY. WHEN YOU BEGIN
TO SEE YOURSELF AS THE "KEY" THAT UNLOCKS
THE MANY POSSIBILITIES, YOUR JOURNEY BECOMES EASIER
YOU ARE THE EXPERIENCE. LOOK CLOSELY AT HOW YOU
WOULD DELETE, ADD, EDIT AND CHANGE
THE SCRIPT OF YOUR LIFE.

DEVELOPING SELF

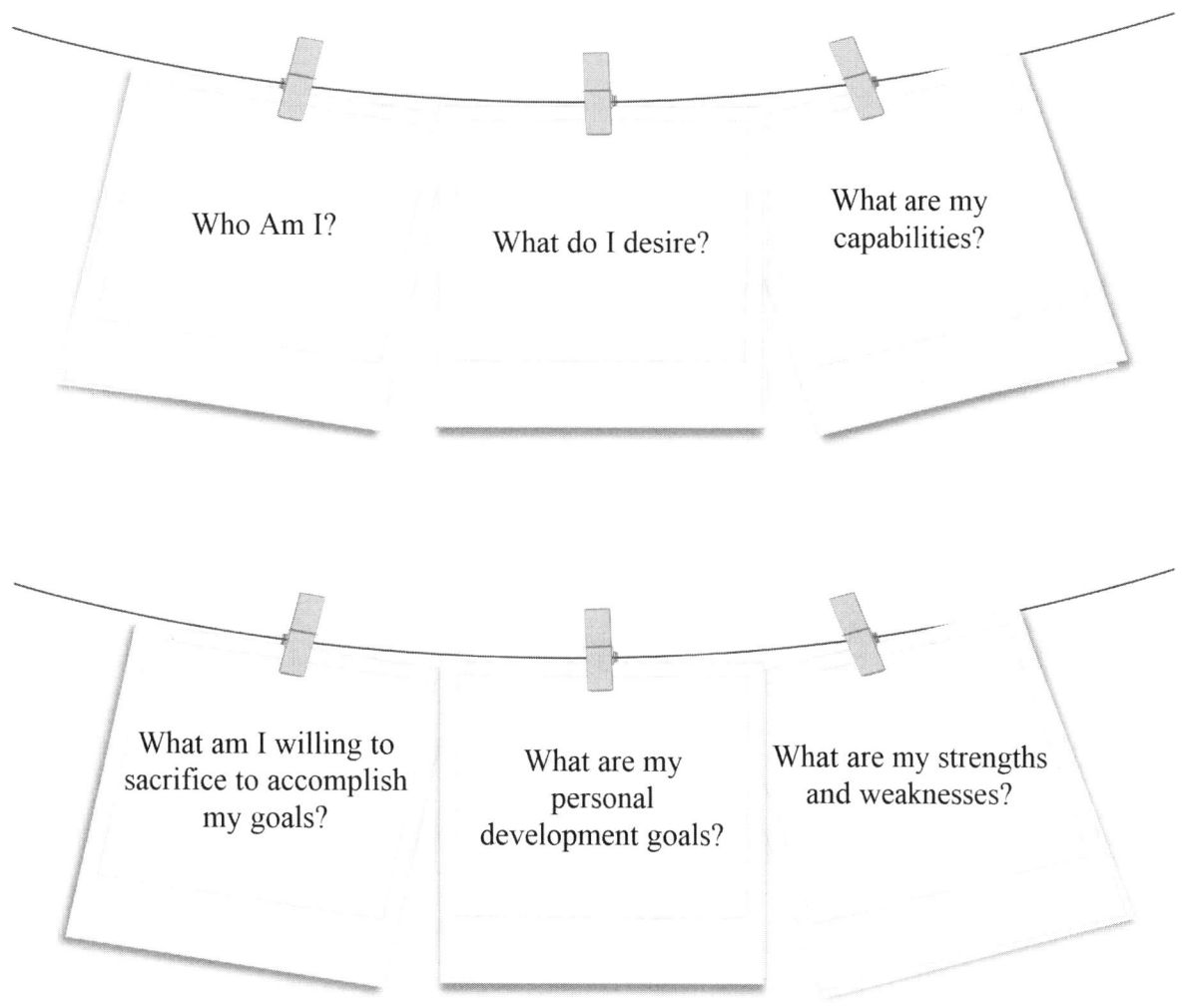

Who Am I?

What do I desire?

What are my capabilities?

What am I willing to sacrifice to accomplish my goals?

What are my personal development goals?

What are my strengths and weaknesses?

Every beginning always has an ending. It's not always going to look pretty, but the only way to see what's at the end is to get started.

What do you need from yourself to begin on this new journey?

_____

_____

_____

_____

_____

_____

_____

_____

_____

_____

_____

_____

_____

_____

_____

ASK YOURSELF:
What are my habits?

When something new is started, it has to be ignited.

The WILL to fuel it is required.

How do you plan on fueling your new beginning and/or your goal(s)?

_____

_____

_____

_____

_____

_____

_____

_____

_____

_____

_____

_____

_____

_____

WHAT IS SOMETHING THAT YOU UNDERSTAND ABOUT YOURSELF THAT YOU WOULD LIKE FOR SOMEONE ELSE TO KNOW?

Personal development, new habits, and self-improvement
are factors for making progress.

In order to make progress towards your goals, what do you intend to change?

_____

_____

_____

_____

_____

_____

_____

_____

_____

_____

_____

_____

_____

WHAT IS ONE THING THAT PEOPLE SAY THAT YOU CAN'T DO?

Respect for the process is a part of success.

**What are some tools you can use to help you develop
patience during the process of success?**

"TO KNOW YOURSELF AS THE BEING UNDERNEATH THE THINKER, THE STILLNESS UNDERNEATH THE MENTAL NOISE, THE LOVE AND JOY UNDERNEATH THE PAIN, IS FREEDOM, SALVATION, ENLIGHTENMENT."

Eckhart Tolle

If you plan for it the best you can, it will come.
**Write down your plans for
achieving your first goal.**

_____

_____

_____

_____

_____

_____

_____

_____

_____

_____

_____

_____

_____

_____

WRITE A LIST OF QUALITIES THAT YOU ADMIRE IN YOURSELF.

Never pay attention to whether life is just or unfair.

Describe and explain life

in your own words.

_____

_____

_____

_____

_____

_____

_____

_____

_____

_____

_____

_____

_____

_____

"YOU SHOULD NOT CHANGE YOURSELF,
BUT CREATE YOURSELF, THAT MEAN BUILD AROUND
YOUR STRENGTHS AND REMOVING BAD HABITS."

Peter F. Drucker

Stay focused on your goals.

**Write down some ways or things that keep you
focused on your goals (List at least 10).**

_____

_____

_____

_____

_____

_____

_____

_____

_____

_____

_____

_____

_____

_____

WHAT DID YOU WANT TO BE GROWING UP? EXPLAIN WHY.

Expect change, it's inevitable.
**Find some things that will help you deal
with change and write them down.**

_____

_____

_____

_____

_____

_____

_____

_____

_____

_____

_____

_____

_____

_____

"YOU SHOULD BE TOO BUSY WATERING YOUR OWN GRASS TO NOTICE IF SOMEONE ELSE'S IS GREENER."

Amy Lee

Keep in mind that your expectations are the death of everything good.

List your personal expectations.

Do you have a plan to navigate them when they don't work?

WHAT ARE 5 ACCOMPLISHMENTS THAT YOU ARE PROUD OF?

We are often in our own way and can prevent ourselves from succeeding.
Name at least five instances where you've messed up a chance to succeed.
Name five things you can do to stop it from happening in the future.

_____

_____

_____

_____

_____

_____

_____

_____

_____

_____

_____

_____

_____

_____

_____

_____

"JOURNALING IS A GREAT WAY TO PAY ATTENTION TO "HOW IT ALL CAME TO BE." IN LOOKING BACK, YOU GAIN INSIGHT INTO (AND APPRECIATION FOR) YOUR CHALLENGES, LESSONS, AND PERSEVERANCE."

Melissa Steginus

Don't settle for things that are not important to you.

Write down all of the things that are important to you.

How can you improve to make them better?

DESCRIBE YOUR FIRST LOVE IN DETAIL.

Hold yourself accountable for your actions and the mistakes you have made.
Name a time when you didn't take responsibility for your actions?
What did you do? How did you fix it?

_____

_____

_____

_____

_____

_____

_____

_____

_____

_____

_____

_____

_____

_____

"YOU WILL NEVER KNOW YOUR FULLEST POTENTIAL, UNLESS YOU ARE FORCED WAY BEYOND YOUR USUAL COMFORT ZONE."

Tony Dovale

Control only what you can and then let go.

**Evaluate your level of control. Write down how you would feel
if you had to give up that level of control.**

WRITE ABOUT A TIME WHEN YOU SABOTAGED YOUR OWN SUCCESS.

Focus on goals that you can control with confidence.
**Write down at least 15 things that will help you
build self-confidence.**

_____

_____

_____

_____

_____

_____

_____

_____

_____

_____

_____

_____

_____

_____

"NOT BEING YOURSELF IS THE WORST FORM OF SELF-DISRESPECT."

Mokokoma Mokhonoana

Learning new things will lead to alternative solutions.

Choose 3 new skills to learn.

Write them down.

_____

_____

_____

_____

_____

_____

_____

_____

_____

_____

_____

_____

_____

_____

_____

_____

WHEN WAS THE LAST TIME YOU FELT LONELY?

Strategize and act with passion.

What are you passionate about?

_____

_____

_____

_____

_____

_____

_____

_____

_____

_____

_____

_____

_____

_____

_____

"BUILD YOURSELF FIRST BEFORE BUILDING RELATIONSHIPS."

Adanne Chukwudi Udejiofor

Goals require action <u>now</u> and reactions <u>later</u>.

What motivates you to take action?

_____

_____

_____

_____

_____

_____

_____

_____

_____

_____

_____

_____

_____

_____

WHAT ARE SOME DECISIONS YOU SHOULD HAVE MADE YESTERDAY ABOUT TODAY?

Be aware of what you are choosing to repeat. Repetition can be a contagious habit.

What are certain things that you do over and over again that are a part of you?

Are they positive, negative, productive etc.?

"BELIEVE THAT YOU WILL SUCCEED,
AND YOU WILL!"

Dilshad Merchant

Make choices by collecting information that will lead to the outcome you want.

Do your choices lead to the outcome(s)

that you desire?

_____

_____

_____

_____

_____

_____

_____

_____

_____

_____

_____

_____

_____

_____

_____

_____

"DICTATE THE ENVIRONMENT YOU WANT TO BE IN. ALWAYS BE AROUND PEOPLE WHO MAKE YOU BETTER. BE AMONGST THOSE WHO INSPIRE YOU."

Janna Cachola

You inform your future, without fear, when you challenge your beliefs.

Recall a time in your life when you challenged your beliefs to achieve your goal(s). Write it down.

_____

_____

_____

_____

_____

_____

_____

_____

_____

_____

_____

_____

_____

_____

WHAT IS <u>ONE</u> CAREER AND <u>ONE</u> LIFE COMPLIMENT THAT YOU'VE EVER RECEIVED?

Don't avoid things that could help you make better choices.

**Who are some of the people who help you
make better choices?**

_____

_____

_____

_____

_____

_____

_____

_____

_____

_____

_____

_____

_____

_____

_____

_____

_____

"AS HUMAN BEINGS, OUR GREATNESS LIES NOT SO MUCH IN BEING ABLE TO REMAKE THE WORLD — THAT IS THE MYTH OF THE ATOMIC — AS IN BEING ABLE TO REMAKE OURSELVES."

Mahatma Gandhi

Your truth is always a strategy to build your success.

What do you want to begin on this new journey?

_____

_____

_____

_____

_____

_____

_____

_____

_____

_____

_____

_____

_____

_____

_____

DESCRIBE BOTH YOUR IDEAL
FRIENDSHIP AND RELATIONSHIP.

Changing your behavior will change your life as well.

Name some events that have taken place in your life that have caused you to change your behavior? Write them down.

_____

_____

_____

_____

_____

_____

_____

_____

_____

_____

_____

_____

_____

_____

_____

"LET HIM WHO WOULD MOVE THE WORLD FIRST MOVE HIMSELF."

Socrates

The outcomes of life determine your willingness to understand yourself.

Write down five consequences (good or bad) that changed your life.

How did they change your life?

_____

_____

_____

_____

_____

_____

_____

_____

_____

_____

_____

_____

_____

_____

_____

_____

_____

WHAT ARE THREE THINGS YOU APPRECIATE MOST ABOUT YOUR LIFE RIGHT NOW? WHY?

Success becomes inevitable when you plan and master your determination.
**Write down a story of success that you are planning
to accomplish in the future.**

_____

_____

_____

_____

_____

_____

_____

_____

_____

_____

_____

_____

_____

_____

_____

"IT IS NOT AS MUCH ABOUT
WHO YOU USED TO BE, AS IT IS
ABOUT WHO YOU CHOOSE TO BE."

Sanhita Baruah

Challenge your norm to gain insight into what could be better.
**Define "norm" in your own words. What are some "norms"
that you could risk to changing this year?**

NAME ONE FAMILY TRADITION THAT YOU WOULD CARRY ON IN THE FUTURE.

Always seek advice but learn to discriminate which input you choose to accept.

What was the best advice that you've ever received?

How do you apply it to your everyday life?

_____

_____

_____

_____

_____

_____

_____

_____

_____

_____

_____

_____

_____

_____

"IF YOU ARE UNDER THE IMPRESSION YOU HAVE ALREADY PERFECTED YOURSELF, YOU WILL NEVER RISE TO THE HEIGHTS YOU ARE NO DOUBT CAPABLE OF."

Kazuo Ishiguro

The Remains of the Day

If you are looking for actual progress, start by changing your way of life.

What are some things you can do differently that

will help you to change as an individual?

_____

_____

_____

_____

_____

_____

_____

_____

_____

_____

_____

_____

_____

_____

WHAT ARE SOME THINGS THAT KEEP YOU UP AT NIGHT?

Failure is an unavoidable pain that facilitates development.
**Create a list of useful items that you can use
when experiencing painful moments.**

"FOR THE BEST RETURN ON YOUR MONEY,
POUR YOUR PURSE INTO YOUR HEAD."

Benjamin Franklin

Courage is confronting what you wish to avoid.

What are some current issues that you want to avoid in life?

Are you planning to confront them either soon or later?

_____

_____

_____

_____

_____

_____

_____

_____

_____

_____

_____

_____

_____

_____

_____

DEFINE SUCCESS. HOW WILL YOU KNOW WHEN YOU HAVE OBTAINED SUCCESS?

Don't underestimate life, it can be very competitive and challenging.
**Write down some of the challenges that you've
experienced over the last year.**

_____

_____

_____

_____

_____

_____

_____

_____

_____

_____

_____

_____

_____

"IF YOU WANT TO CHANGE THE FRUITS,
YOU WILL FIRST HAVE TO CHANGE THE ROOTS.
IF YOU WANT TO CHANGE THE VISIBLE,
YOU MUST FIRST CHANGE THE INVISIBLE."

T. Harv Eker

Secrets of the Millionaire Mind:
Mastering the Inner Game of Wealth

Improvements can only come through action.

What are some improvements you can make to your life, and what action would you take to make those improvements?

_____

_____

_____

_____

_____

_____

_____

_____

_____

_____

_____

_____

_____

_____

_____

_____

_____

_____

DESCRIBE WHAT YOUR PERFECT DAY LOOKS LIKE.

Rejection is a universal fear that many are trying to avoid.

Write down a time when you were rejected.

How did you react to the rejection?

"THE MIND IS JUST LIKE A MUSCLE —
THE MORE YOU EXERCISE IT, THE STRONGER
IT GETS AND THE MORE IT CAN EXPAND."

Idowu Koyenikan

Wealth for All: Living a Life of Success at the Edge of Your Ability

Change the choices that don't work for you.
What are some choices you have made repeatedly
that you need to change?

WHAT IS ONE THING BESIDES MONEY THAT WOULD MAKE YOUR LIFE EASIER?

It is the nature of the human being to be a student of all things.

Create a list of things that you would like to learn

in the next two years.

"ALL OF OUR KNOWLEDGE HAS ITS ORIGIN IN OUR PERCEPTIONS."

Leonardo Da Vinci

Work on influencing yourself, and while doing so, consider paying attention to yourself.
Pay attention to how you influence yourself when
you're dealing with everyday life.

WHAT WOULD YOU LIKE TO BE DOING WITH YOUR LIFE RIGHT NOW?

Time and action will determine the outcome.

Schedule a date and time when you will start your first goal.

Explain what actions you are going to take to achieve that goal in writing.

_____

_____

_____

_____

_____

_____

_____

_____

_____

_____

_____

_____

_____

_____

_____

"WE MUST BECOME WHAT WE WISH TO TEACH."

Nathaniel Branden

Six Pillars of Self-Esteem

Model the things that you desire.

Name at last three role models that inspire you.

Why do they inspire you?

_____

_____

_____

_____

_____

_____

_____

_____

_____

_____

_____

_____

_____

_____

LIST SOME OF THE ISSUES THAT YOU GET INTO THE MOST ARGUMENTS ABOUT.

Through your choices, learn to accept all the experiences you create.

What are some of the experiences you've learned

from the choices you made?

_____

_____

_____

_____

_____

_____

_____

_____

_____

_____

_____

_____

_____

_____

_____

"THE HUMAN SPIRIT WILL NOT INVEST ITSELF IN A COMPROMISE."

Robert Fritz

The Path of Least Resistance:
Learning to Become the Creative Force in Your Own Life

There is a solution to every problem that exists.

Take the time today to help somebody find a solution to their problem.

Write about how you helped them solve their problem.

_____

_____

_____

_____

_____

_____

_____

_____

_____

_____

_____

_____

_____

_____

_____

_____

WHAT ARE SOME POSITIVE THINGS THAT YOU COULD LEARN FROM YOUR COMMUNITY?

Embrace your challenges as much as you embrace your achievements.
**Name a moment in which you encountered a challenge that
ultimately led to a future achievement.**

_____

_____

_____

_____

_____

_____

_____

_____

_____

_____

_____

_____

_____

_____

"IF YOU WANT TO LEAD AN EXTRAORDINARY LIFE, FIND OUT WHAT THE ORDINARY DO — AND DON'T DO IT."

Tommy Newberry

Success is Not an Accident:
Change Your Choices Change Your Life

Hold yourself accountable for your responsibilities.
**What responsibilities are you currently not
holding yourself accountable for?**

_____

_____

_____

_____

_____

_____

_____

_____

_____

_____

_____

_____

_____

_____

WHAT ARE SOME THINGS THAT YOU NEED TO ACCOMPLISH BY THE END OF THE YEAR TO MAKE IT MEANINGFUL?

Change is a significant option.

Look up some of the options that can help you change in one area of your life.

Name those options and how you will apply them to your life.

_____

_____

_____

_____

_____

_____

_____

_____

_____

_____

_____

_____

_____

_____

_____

"IT'S TIME TO REFLECT ON
WHAT YOU WANT TO DO — TO DISCOVER
WHAT MATTERS MOST TO YOU."

Tamara S. Raymond

Control is as addictive as a drug.

What are some control issues that you can't let go of?

How are they affecting your life?

ARE THERE ANY PEOPLE IN YOUR LIFE
THAT YOU ENVY PROFESSIONALLY?
IF SO, WHY AND HAVE YOU TRIED
DUPLICATING THEIR PATTERNS?

Carefully choose your response to provoking reactions.

**Take the time today to respond carefully
to other people's reactions.**

"DON'T PROCRASTINATE, START BUILDING YOURSELF NOW!"

Sunday Adelaja

Everyday decisions and choices define who you are to others as an individual.

How do you feel about your decision-making?

What are some ways you can make better choices?

_____

_____

_____

_____

_____

_____

_____

_____

_____

_____

_____

_____

_____

_____

_____

_____

_____

ARE YOU STILL CARRYING OLD PAIN?

IF SO, RESEARCH WAYS YOU CAN LEARN TO LET IT GO.

Move urgently toward the things you desire with purpose.

What motivates you to move towards your "Why"?

"YOUR SELF-TALK IS THE CHANNEL OF BEHAVIOR CHANGE."

Gino Norris

Create meaningful daily internal dialogues.
**Write down at least 20 affirmations that can be used
for your personal internal dialogue.**

IF YOU COULD GO BACK, WHAT ARE SOME THINGS
THAT YOU WOULD CHANGE ABOUT YOUR LIFE?
WHY WOULD YOU CHANGE IT?

Attention is the price that must be paid for all things.

What price are you willing to pay for the things

that you desire or want to achieve?

"MAN IS NOT GOING TO WAIT PASSIVELY FOR MILLIONS OF YEARS BEFORE EVOLUTION OFFERS HIM A BETTER BRAIN."

Corneliu E. Giurgea

Have optimism, even knowing that what is unfamiliar will bring fear and discomfort.
During times of discomfort, what brings you joy?

_____

_____

_____

_____

_____

_____

_____

_____

_____

_____

_____

_____

_____

_____

_____

_____

DESCRIBE "GOD" IN YOUR OWN WORDS.

Manage your daily behavioral experiences and it will allow you to communicate with others with a purposeful attitude. **When communicating with others when you are upset, how do you manage your behavior?**

"WHAT WE FEAR DOING MOST IS USUALLY WHAT WE MOST NEED TO DO."

Ralph Waldo Emerson

The problems you point out in others can often be found within you.
Today, self-reflect and journal what you've been reflecting on.

WHAT RELATIONSHIPS DO YOU CURRENTLY HAVE THAT ARE DRAINING YOU?

Invest in tools that will help you commit to future success.

What book(s) are you currently reading?

_____

_____

_____

_____

_____

_____

_____

_____

_____

_____

_____

_____

_____

_____

_____

_____

"TREAT A MAN AS HE IS AND HE WILL REMAIN AS HE IS. TREAT A MAN AS CAN AND SHOULD BE AND HE WILL BECOME AS HE CAN AND SHOULD BE."

Stephen R. Covey

Excuses purposely dodge results.
**Name a few excuses that you use to
get away from doing things.**

_____

_____

_____

_____

_____

_____

_____

_____

_____

_____

_____

_____

_____

_____

_____

WRITE ABOUT THE TIME WHEN YOU FELT
YOU BECAME A "GROWN-UP".

Limited beliefs are detrimental to individual results.

Identify some of your limited beliefs.

Identify some ways that you can overcome these limited beliefs.

"CHOOSE TO BE
THE BEST VERSION OF YOU."

Truth Devour

Become a student of good plans and concepts.
Are you currently enrolled in a course that
can help you develop yourself?

_____

_____

_____

_____

_____

_____

_____

_____

_____

_____

_____

_____

_____

_____

_____

WHAT IS AN EXPERIENCE ABOUT LIFE
THAT YOU WOULD LIKE TO FORGET?

Patience is a key element of success.

Define patience and success in your own words.

_____

_____

_____

_____

_____

_____

_____

_____

_____

_____

_____

_____

_____

_____

_____

_____

"ADDING LITTLE AMOUNTS OVER TIME MAKES A HUGE DIFFERENCE."

Leo Babauta

Your imagination is a powerful resource and the creator of all things possible.

List some of the resources that you would recommend to others to use.

Why are the resources useful?

WHERE IS ONE PLACE IN THE WORLD THAT
YOU WOULD LIKE TO TRAVEL? WHY?

Ignorance is not a worthwhile alternative.

What are some ways that you can make life worthwhile for somebody?

_____

_____

_____

_____

_____

_____

_____

_____

_____

_____

_____

_____

_____

_____

_____

"JUST ABOUT ANY PERSONALITY TRAIT OR SKILL CAN BE LEARNED: SIMPLY FIND IT IN SOMEONE YOU KNOW AND COPY IT. THEN WATCH WHAT HAPPENS."

Steve Goodier

Discipline is the practice of a consistent habit.

List a minimum of 10 good and bad habits you have.

_____

_____

_____

_____

_____

_____

_____

_____

_____

_____

_____

_____

_____

_____

_____

_____

WHAT IS ONE CHANGE THAT YOU WOULD MAKE, IF YOU HAD THE OPPORTUNITY TO RUN THE COUNTRY FOR A DAY? WHY?

Always be encouraged to live out your dreams.
Write down and compare the dreams of
your childhood and adulthood.

_____

_____

_____

_____

_____

_____

_____

_____

_____

_____

_____

_____

_____

_____

_____

_____

"I BELIEVE IN KNOWING WHO YOU ARE BUT WITHOUT LIMITING YOURSELF TO YOUR OWN EXPECTATION OF WHO YOU ARE."

Charlotte Eriksson

128

Build your own success model.

Who is your model of success and why?

_____

_____

_____

_____

_____

_____

_____

_____

_____

_____

_____

_____

_____

_____

_____

_____

WHAT LIFE ADVICE WOULD YOU GIVE TO YOUR YOUNGER SELF?

Only educate yourself about the things you're willing to learn.

Are you open to learning new things?

If so, how do you know?

_____

_____

_____

_____

_____

_____

_____

_____

_____

_____

_____

_____

_____

_____

"WE ARE ALL BORN WITH EXTRAORDINARY POWERS OF IMAGINATION, INTELLIGENCE, FEELING, INTUITION, SPIRITUALITY, AND OF PHYSICAL AND SENSORY AWARENESS.

Ken Robinson

Survive the first 30 days and success is bound to follow.
**How long does it take for you to unlearn and learn
a new habit from an old habit?**

_____

_____

_____

_____

_____

_____

_____

_____

_____

_____

_____

_____

_____

_____

WHAT HOBBY MAKES YOU FEEL THE HAPPIEST?

Take advantage of the moments that support your goals.
**List moments from individuals who
help support your goals.**

_____

_____

_____

_____

_____

_____

_____

_____

_____

_____

_____

_____

_____

_____

_____

_____

"USING YOUR IMAGINATION MEANS THAT YOU ARE USING YOUR MOST POWERFUL TOOL OF CREATION, MANIFESTATION AND MODIFICATION."

Dorothy Holder

Pay attention to your opportunities because they have an expiration date.

List the opportunities you've received this month.

_____

_____

_____

_____

_____

_____

_____

_____

_____

_____

_____

_____

_____

_____

_____

_____

NAME ONE THING THAT YOU'D NEVER DO
AND EXPLAIN WHY.

Model those who produce visible results.

Define the term "outcome" in your own words.

"GROWTH IS NEVER AN EVENT, IT'S A PROCESS."

Ifeanyi Enoch Onuoha

You cannot change things that you refuse to acknowledge.

Define "change" and how it applies to you.

_____

_____

_____

_____

_____

_____

_____

_____

_____

_____

_____

_____

_____

_____

_____

WHAT ARE THE THINGS THAT YOU ARE MOST GRATEFUL FOR?

Be who you are but be willing to make some adjustments.
Are you operating in your true, authentic self at the moment?
Explain your way of knowing.

_____

_____

_____

_____

_____

_____

_____

_____

_____

_____

_____

_____

_____

_____

_____

_____

"WHEN WE KNOW OUR TRUE NATURE, ESPECIALLY THE FUNCTIONING OF THE MIND, WE STOP BEING JUDGMENTAL AND BECOME AN INSPIRATION AND SUPPORT TO OTHERS."

Thomas Vazhakunnathu

The objective is to know what you want before you pursue it.

Create a vision board for the things you want.

_____

_____

_____

_____

_____

_____

_____

_____

_____

_____

_____

_____

_____

IF THERE WAS ONE PERSON YOU COULD WRITE A LETTER TO TODAY, WHO WOULD IT BE? WHY?

Forgiveness is a conscious choice we make to create emotional freedom.
Take the time today to forgive someone
who has hurt you.

"YOUR VISION WILL BECOME CLEAR
ONLY WHEN YOU LOOK INTO YOUR HEART.
WHO LOOKS OUTSIDE, WISHES. WHO LOOKS INSIDE,
FINDS INFINITE WISDOM."

Sereda Aleta Dailey

Reciprocate what others are willing to do for you.

Do something nice for someone today.

NAME ONE THING THAT YOU ARE MOST AFRAID OF LOSING. WHAT WOULD YOU BE LOSING IF YOU LOST THIS ONE THING?

Unlearn what will no longer serve your higher good.
Write down and then let go of the things that
will no longer serve your higher good.

What are three qualities that you possess and would share with others?

Qualities

_____

_____

_____

Write down at least three of your strengths and three weaknesses.

Weaknesses

_____

_____

_____

Strengths

_____

_____

_____

What are three personality traits that define you?

How can you use these traits to help you be successful in any area of your life?

Personality Traits

_____

_____

_____

Evaluate your life, and where you are with the truth.

When was the last time you told yourself the truth about a situation?

What was that truth?

_____

_____

_____

_____

_____

_____

_____

_____

_____

_____

_____

_____

_____

_____

"KNOWING HIGHER TRUTHS ENSURE THAT WE HAVE A LARGER PERSPECTIVE WHERE ALL OTHER THINGS FALL IN PLACE OR START MAKING SENSE."

Thomas Vazhakunnathu

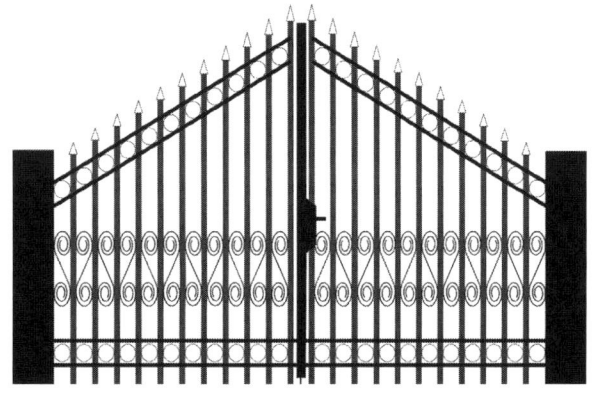